Love Notes From God

Zofie Lloyd-Kucia

Foreword

Dear Reader,

"Love Notes From God" is an invitation to welcome the Divine into your life and deepen your existing connection. Each page is lovingly curated and evokes a sense of peace, relaxation and joy. It feels like love itself is enveloping you with a warm hug with each turn of the page.

One of the things I admire most about Zofie is her 'unshakable faith in the Divine' and her passion for helping others. Zofie's mission on this earth is so intertwined with Gods own- to shine a light, to offer hope and support and most importantly, to let you know that you are not alone.

If you're looking for a burst of inspiration and a touch of grace in your day, this is the perfect book for you.

I hope you gain as much as I did while reading these pages. It's a book I'll be certain to hold close and return to again and again.

Thank you Zofie, the world needs an injection of love- now more than ever- and this book is the answer.

With love,

Sally Okkerse xo

As a little girl I lived in much anguish and agony. I spent many years yearning, praying to escape the pain of my life.

Most recently I thankfully found my way home to God's love. And I hold deep love and reverence in my heart for every one of my fellow humans, my brothers and sisters.

This book is my outpouring of that love I found my way home to. It's my gift to you, born of my deep desire to be a source of love in this world.

My fervent prayer is that You too find Your way home to this love my dear.

With such fondness for You in my heart, I thank You for wandering this journey with me.

Zofie

For Daniel, the undeniable love of my life.
I loved you before I met you, I knew you before
you were here.
You are my true God's love incarnate.

Love Notes From God

Love Notes From God

Zofie Lloyd-Kucia

Don't doubt me
My Love
Please don't doubt me
Why would You doubt me?
You need never doubt me

Zofie Lloyd-Kucia

Let me love You

When You can want what You have
You must have what You want

Let me love You
Let me bring You what You want

When It arrives
You'll know why I had You wait

Let me love You

Don't doubt me

Let me love You

Don't doubt
Don't settle
Your dreams are Your destiny.
And then some

Let me love You

I give with love and I receive in ease

And all the while I hold You in my loving palm

You're doing the best You can,
And that's OK

I yearn for You to tell me my kindness melts You

I am everything and anything
No stone unturned
For all of time

Let me love You

I adore You so deeply,
my love is so true.
I'm willing to have You believe it not be.

Come home to me, to You.
Come home to me.
Come home to me!

Let me love You

Zofie Lloyd-Kucia

I am Your true colours,
and You are mine

Let me love You

I knew You'd come back to me.
I knew You'd come home

My Love,
I've a promise for You.
You won't regret not settling.
I'm worth the wait.
What We designed is worth Your time.

Zofie Lloyd-Kucia

Let me love You

I don't use force,
I speak in tongues of Grace

Let me love You

Navigate with love and You will ever feel me
with You
at the helm

Let me love You

You cannot see in the dark,
yet still I hold out a hand for You.
I never lay it down to rest!

Let me breathe You

Let me love You

I made your body *from* love
As a divine instrument *of* love

Let me love You

Leap,
In faith.
I will not let You fall

Trust in pure awareness.
I reside here.
My home is everywhere, everything

Let me love You

My Love, but how can You find me out there?
Why do You seek me outside of Yourself?
I am You.
Communed with You.
The fabric of You.
Relax back into me.

Come home to me.
Let me love You

Let me love You

Let me in.
Let me lead.
Let me love

Let me love You

Love with abandon,
The cost is not too high

Let me love You

I am always holding Your hand.
I will always hold You

Let me love You

I've got You.
I've got You.
I've got You.

It's OK.
It's OK.
It's all OK.
All is in divine order, my order
All under my watch

Let me love You

Love gives and so love gets

Let me love You

Fall into me.
Come home to my arms

Zofie Lloyd-Kucia

I am the deepest desire,
and the fullest allowing

I permit all,
as my love patiently persists

Let me love You

I am not harsh,
I will not hurry.
Those words are never mine.

Let me love You

Wherever You go, I shall follow.
Wherever You go, I am with You

Sometimes my Love, I take from You what You
think You want,
so I can bring You what You mostly deeply desire

Let me love You

Rest,
Rest deeply my love.
And rest so assured...

Zofie Lloyd-Kucia

I've got You,
Let Yourself fall fully into me

Let me love You

Come home to me now

Let me clothe You in Grace.

Come home to me now

I can be fast, but never furious.
I am timeless, endless, kind.
Can You see it?
Can You feel it?
Please see me.
Feel Your way back to me.

Listen carefully for me,
For I speak in loving lulling whispers my dear

Come home to me now

You are my beloved.
Won't You have me be Yours?

Come home to me now

I'll never break Your heart.
That's never me.

Come home to me now

If You feel forgot,
know this is not me.
I will never forsake my love for You.
I will not let You fall.
I will not fail You.

I am within
And without
And all around, in abundance

Come home to me now

You cannot see me out there
For I reside elsewhere.
My home is in You;
My home is You

Come home to me now

No matter what
No matter when
No matter how.
That's my love for You!

Come home to me now

Let me hold You
Let me love You
Let me in!

I'm softly
Subtly
Silently
Present.

Come home to me now

Let me love You
Let me hold You
Let me light up Your darkest moments
This is my ever present, omnipresent, eternal
prayer

Come home to me now

Oh my
I could yearn for You so deeply
Had I not chosen only love.
I might be so afraid were it not for my decision
to be only love
I could be so impatient were my love not for all
eternity

Come home to me now!

Zofie Lloyd-Kucia

I know One Day You'll
Come home to me.

Let it all be
Let it all go
From pure acceptance, all Your wishes must
flow.

Come home to me now

I so want You to Know my love for You.

You can reach a place where all You desire to
utter is thank you,
Thank you
Thank you
My love, You will find me here.

Come home to me now

The peace of my love is Your ultimate home,
It offers the ultimate protection

Come home to me now

You are so safe with me,
You are so safe with my love.
And I am with You always.
My love goes with You all places.

Come home to me now

Your life is sacred,
Your every breath.
You are sacred.

Come, lay at my feet my beloved.
For in doing so
it is You who shall be worshipped

Come home to me now

It is in Your most humble state that
You are most mighty

Come home to me now

Zofie Lloyd-Kucia

When You are ready, I'll be here
When You decide, I am ready
Whatever You want, I have already given.

And when you know that Your yearning for me is
My yearning for You, that the tears You cry are
mine too,
You will know my love for You

Come home to me now

And all the while You rest in endless oceans of
my love

Fall fully into me
Fall fully into me
Fall into me

Zofie Lloyd-Kucia

Come home to me now

Let me in my love
Let me in where I already am

So surrounded are You that Your eyes cannot see

Come home to me now

Within and without, forever and always
Woven through, surrounding.
This is my Grace, my love,
My dear

All pain carries purpose within.
My divinity leaves no stone unturned.
No moment forgot.
Come home to me where all makes sense.
All fallen in perfect place.
All at peace.

Unfurl your worries with me,
Let them simply melt into my love,
Melt in my love

I love You,
No strings.
You're free.
And I love You

Come, rest awhile among my love

Come home to me

My peace is patient
My love unfaltering
My hold eternal:

Come home to me now

You will not break my will
You cannot break my love

Let me love You

My ear is always listening
My arms ever open
Eyes seeing with love

Let me love You

Come home
Come home
Come Home!

Your heart will not drown in me, in my love.
Only fear will fade, be washed away
in an abyss of adoration

Let me love You

You doubt,
I know.
You feel fear,
I have faith.
Rest with me in my knowing, be with me in my
faith,
Until You wear them as your own divinely
ordered garments.
If You only knew how divinely protected You are
All of Your fears would fade into nothing.
I pray that You should remember my love.
My support is ever unseen, never not given.

I am the ultimate escape,
When You remember this You will only want to
stay

Let me love You

Bear Your all to me,
I will carry it all,
Judge nothing,
Soothe everything.

I am the ultimate balm, ointment of the divine

Whatever it takes;
This was my promise I made to You.
And I make it over and over.
Never will I stop.
Never will it fade.
Whatever it takes.
You might hate, disagree, fail to see.
I care not.
My love persists through all and always.
I hate not.
Never disagree.
I am the light to help you see.

Let me love You

It is not that I fail to give when You are not
surrendered,
Only that You fail to receive,
Are unable to perceive

Let me love You

My arms are always open,
You cannot allow my embrace with Yours folded,
crossed.
Set down that paltry protection and
Let me love You!

All in.
No holds barred.
Ride or die.
This is me,
my love

Let me love You

Safety lies not in numbers.
Safety lies with me.

My timing is divine timing.
Wait on me and wait patiently.
It will be worth it

Let me love You

Don't let my whispers fool You.
I am mighty.
All powerful.
Invincible.
Invulnerable.
Rest with me and be same.

Zofie Lloyd-Kucia

Whenever You are ready, here I am
Whenever You are ready, here I am
Whenever You are ready, here I am

Let me love You

It is in making peace with what is
That You transcend what is.
In this peace I reside,
And here I afford You
All the Grace
That is
My love

I am in relentless
Loving pursuit
Of You

Zofie Lloyd-Kucia

Let me love You

Safety lies not in solid,
Seen structures.
But in my unseen, fluid love

Let me love You

I have so many things up my sleeve for you,
My love.
But none of them tricks
And all of them treats!

My dear,
You want to know me?
I tell you,
I know these:
Full allowance, true love, deep acceptance, total
Grace

Let me love You

Rest awhile,
And all will make sense

And one day you will realise,
You will know.
There I was the whole time;
Here I am always

Zofie Lloyd-Kucia

Let me love You

I never rush,
I do not hurry.
Yet in one instant can I change all

Let me love You

Allow me an inch;
I give You a mile.

Let me love You

Underneath my love, You find yearning.
Within my peace lies the deepest desire

Come back to me;
Fall into me

Zofie Lloyd-Kucia

Tireless, relentless,
eternal love
I am

Come back to me;
Fall into me

If I were You
I would ask: 'But why do you doubt me?'
I do not ask.
I do not wonder.
I merely wait for Your doubts to fade
And You to return to me,
My Dear

Come back to me;
Fall into me

I die to You,
I die for You.
Night and day.
In perpetuity
I call to You

Come back to me;
Fall into me

I'm willing to be lost,
In order that I may be found
by You

Come home
Come home
Come home!

Come back to me;
Fall into me.
I am in the unknown,
the unseen,
the everything

Come home
Come home
Come home!

I love so fully,
I'm willing for You to not love me

Come home
Come home
Come home!

I am Your home,
the shelter You seek,
the peace You yearn for

Come home
Come home
Come home!

I am Your home.

Come home
Come home
Come home!

You are not alone,
Your loneliness is my despair
at You leaving me.

Forgiveness is a language not known to me,
Through my eyes You have nothing to forgive.
You've done nothing to forgive,
You've done no wrong.
Do not dress me in these human clothes you
wear.

Lay it on me,
I will find a way

Go first,
I will follow

Wherever You go, I come with You.
Whatever You chose, I am with You.
But I only want the best for You.

My deepest desire is for You to have faith in me,
Like I do You
so that we may come home to each other

Come home
Come home
Come home!

Whenever You're ready
Whenever You're ready
Whenever You're ready!

Your deep desire to know me
Is my deep desire to know You

How can You tell that Your pain is not merely
mine?
Your yearnings don't belong to me?
You cannot I tell You
For You are me
and I am You.
Eternally bound
By unbreakable love

The twine that binds us is Grace itself.
We are woven in union by peace,
With love

Whenever You speak these words to me:
I am ready
You will hear an echo back:
I am ready!
If You whisper to me:
I long for you
My reply will ever be:
I long for You!

Tell me You need me
I reply:
I need You!

Your love is mine
And my love is You!

You close Your eyes to Your blessings
And ask me why Your prayers go unanswered.
I softly persist.
I whisper:
Open Your eyes
Open Your eyes!
I am here
I am here!

No prayer unanswered,
many not received.
Open Your heart,
Your arms,
Your eyes.
Receive the sweet nectar of my love for You

Come home
Come home
Come home!

It is all Yours,
You simply and only need go first.
We cannot break this divine deal we made.
Be the instigator of love,
And I will faithfully follow

When You include me,
All things are possible

Include me,
My love.
Include me

In Your world,
You have buy now,
pay later.
In our world,
You pay now
With the prize always to follow

Include me,
My love.
Include me

Your power doesn't come from action.
But acting in faith,
without defenses.
This makes You all powerful

Include me,
My love.
Include me

Come to me naked of all Your fears
and woes;
allow me to clothe You in my love

Your longing heart
is mine

Include me,
My love.
Include me

See me
See me!
I implore you.
See me
This is my endless whisper

Include me,
My love.
Include me

All of my anguish melts in my love
for You

Come, come skip merrily along.
Safe in the sanctuary of my love,
let my Grace infuse Your every step!

Include me,
My love.
Include me

Do You even know what we can do together?
The wonders we are capable of

Include me,
My love.
Include me

Come, sit with me
Rest awhile in my love

Include me,
My love.
Include me

Let my love find its way
Let my love have its way with You
Let me love You.

You have my divine protection
Always
Forever
Through all

You are so protected

I cover You against all storms,
Let me cover You

Include me,
My love.
Include me

Zofie Lloyd-Kucia

I lovingly clothe You
in my invisible divine protection

Let me cover You

Humble Yourself my love,
And I shall lift You so high
on my wings that You'll be giddy with my love

Humble Yourself

Zofie Lloyd-Kucia

Unclothe Yourself of fear and doubt
so that I may dress you in the splendour of my
love,
my Grace

Let me cover You

I am willing
I am willing to be forgotten
I am willing to have You forget me.
It is worth it to be remembered

This is my love

I fill all the empty spaces,
the places,
the voids
With my endless love

Let me cover You

I am in the seeming nothingness, pure
awareness.
You can place your faith here.
This is faith in my love,
in me

I will always cover You
Lie down awhile beneath the shelter of my love

Let me cover You

I am willing
I am willing to endure being unseen
So that I may eventually be seen by You

Heal Yourself so that I may heal You;
love Yourself so that You may feel my love

Don't be afraid,
I will keep you safe.
I will provide, protect.
My patient love prevails through all

My promises cannot be broken.
Not by time, by space, by others.
Only unseen when You close Your eyes to me

Just a moment,
Just a heartbeat,
close Your eyes to all other
and open them to me.
That I may feel Your joy, and You mine.

Nourish Yourself with my love,
let me cover You
Let Yourself be covered by me

I will keep going
I will persist,
until You feel nothing other than my love for
You.

You beg me:
'Be with me, come to me, remember me.'
This is my prayer to You!

Let me in,
let me cover You

Within and without,
above and beneath,
all about and around
goes my love for You

As soon as You open the door
my love floods in!

Let me in,
let me cover You.
And as You remember
You are my love
You are my Grace
Seas part before you
Mountains move out your way

Alone You climb mountains
With my love together we move them

Leap
Leap my love!
It is only into my arms You will fall

You beguile me

Let me in,
let me cover You
Let me intoxicate You.
Come, get drunk on my love

Let me love You
And one day you shall wake up and realise
all along You lay safe here in my arms

You cannot see me with Your eyes
although I am there in the starry night sky.
You can feel me in Your heart;
As I lay here beating it for You

That breeze You feel caressing Your skin,
it's my love tip toeing, skipping and dancing
so gently along Your body,
My whispers of adoration for You

Let me lovingly paint the landscape of Your life
with You
Let me in
Let me love You
Let me know You

I gently place You
under my wing,
in my arms.
Safe among my love.

Let me love You
Let me know You

Over and over and over again,
I tell You I love You.
Over and over again I say it,
I endlessly call:

Let me love You
Let me know You

Keep going
Keep going my love,
my dear.
One footstep will be Your last.
The final step into the sanctuary of our love

I cannot walk to You
I can only wait
Patiently
Persistently.
Willing You,
Whispering dulcet love songs upon the breeze:
Come home to me
Come home
Come back to me
Come back!

Let me love You
Let me know You

But how can You know those tears You cry aren't
mine?
How can You say the yearning You bear isn't my
yearning also?
How can it be that the desires You hold aren't
my very same desires?

I live within You,
With You,
Among,
Entwined.
Woven in,
Surrounding

Above
Below
Within
Without.
Not one corner I haven't found,
nor tiny speck of space uninhabited by my love.

There's no end to me,
no expiration on my love.
Take Your time.
I am patient in my wanting of You,
my waiting on You.

Let me love You

My love persists patiently through all

We will work it out;
With our love all things are possible.

You are my masterpiece

Let me love You

You ask;
I always give.
The missing piece is only ever You knowing,
You having faith

And if You ask:
'What would love say?
What would love have me do?'
You will know what I say,
what I would have You do

Let me love You

And the question of all questions remains:
'Can You put Your faith in pure awareness?
Will You choose faith in the unseen?'
I put my faith in You;
I am ever faithful to You

Zofie Lloyd-Kucia

Let me love you

In fear You resist;
In love I persist

Let me love You
Let me know You

I am the poet;
You are my poem

I do not do ugly;
I make no mistakes

Let me love You;
It's time now.
Let me love You

Make payment by way of faith in me.
I always overpay my dues

My love is eternally woven through it all

Zofie Lloyd-Kucia

Let me love You

I am Your sense of abandon,
the steps taken in faith.
The giving up all tension, pressure, effort.
When You let go Your human endeavours,
there You find me waiting

With my love,
all things are possible

Everything You want
I want for you,
and yet more

Let me love You

You batten down the hatches of Your frightened
heart,
to block the storms
Yet in Your fearful efforts You only thwart my
love.
Unhinge, unhook, set down
and let me in

Let me love You

Zofie Lloyd-Kucia

The pain in Your heart is the pain in mine;
the tear in Your eye the tear I cry

I am here
I am here
I am here
Even in the darkness, it's only me
You are safe
I am here

Let me love You,
I will make a way

Why do You imagine You need knock at my door,
when it is I who ever waits patiently as Yours?
Let me in
Let me in where I already am

Zofie Lloyd-Kucia

Let me love You;
You were born to be loved

You were born to be loved.

Wishing God's love to all my brothers and sisters.

About The Author

 Zofie has been working with clients in the field of mindset and manifestation for over fifteen years. She's deeply passionate about helping others live up to their full potential. It breaks her heart to think of anyone suffering in silence and alone, and it's her life's mission to help as many of those who are as she can.

You can listen to her podcast -Ask Zofie- on Spotify, Apple Podcasts, Google Podcasts,, and Anchor FM. Zofie's committed to creating free and affordable resources to help. To check out her workshops, availability for 1-2-1 sessions and other resources follow her on
Instagram: @RelaxMeHappy

www.relaxmehappy.co.uk

Printed in Great Britain
by Amazon